COUNTRIES OF THE WORLD

GERMANY

SONJA SCHANZ AND GERRY DONALDSON

Facts On File, Inc.

TITLES IN THE COUNTRIES OF THE WORLD SERIES:
AUSTRALIA • BRAZIL • CHINA • EGYPT • FRANCE • GERMANY • ITALY
JAPAN • KENYA • MEXICO • UNITED KINGDOM • UNITED STATES

Germany

Copyright © 2004 by Evans Brothers Limited

Facts On File, Inc.
132 West 31st Street
New York NY 10001

Library of Congress Cataloging-in-Publication Data

Schanz, Sonja.
  Germany / Sonja Schanz and Gerry Donaldson
    p. cm. — (Countries of the world)
  Originally published: London: Evans Brothers, c2004.
  ISBN 0-8160-5501-7 (hc)
  1. Germany—Juvenile literature. I. Donaldson, Gerry,
1944– II. Title. III. Countries of the world (Facts On File,
Inc.)

DD17.S27 2004
943—dc22   2004045434

Facts On File books are available at special discounts
when purchased in bulk quantities for businesses,
associations, institutions, or sales promotions. Please
call our Special Sales Department in New York at
(212) 967-8800 or (800) 322-8755.

You can find Facts On File on the World Wide Web at
http://www.factsonfile.com.

Printed in China by Imago

10 9 8 7 6 5 4 3 2 1

Endpapers (front): Schloss Neuschwanstein
in the German Alps (Bavaria).
Title page: Tourists in Heidelberg.
Imprint and Contents page: Reconstructed buildings in
the war-damaged city of Dresden.
Endpapers (back): The skyline of Frankfurt.

Editor: Susie Brooks
Designer: Jane Hawkins
Map artwork: Peter Bull
Charts and graphs: Encompass Graphics, Ltd.
Photographs: all by Nigel Hicks except front
                     endpapers (Corbis Digital Stock);
                     15 (Peter Usbeck, Alamy); 19
                     (Image Works, Topham
                     Picturepoint); 33 top (Robert
                     Bosch, GmbH); 50 (Marcus Matzel,
                     Still Pictures); 52 (Andreas Buck,
                     Still Pictures).

First published by Evans Brothers Limited, 2A Portman
Mansions, Chiltern Street, London W1U 6NR, United
Kingdom.

This edition published under license from Evans Brothers
Limited. All rights reserved.

The Federal Republic of
Germany is represented
by a black, red and gold
striped flag.

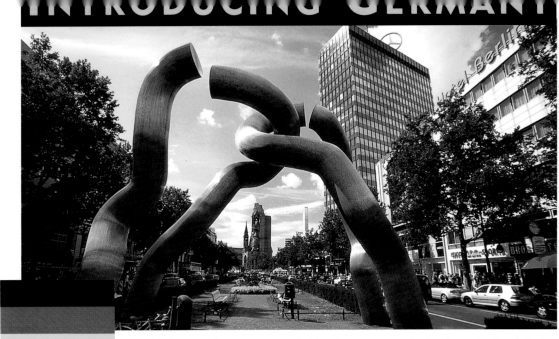

Modern architecture surrounds historic monuments in the dynamic city of Berlin.

Germany lies in the heart of Europe, sharing a border with nine other countries. It is the third-largest country in Western Europe (after France and Spain) and the greatest in terms of population. Germany is a relatively young country, but it has a complex history.

— Main roads
----- Railways
✈ International airports

A DISJOINTED PAST

Germany did not exist until 1871, when various separate kingdoms, dukedoms and city-states were unified to create a single nation. Prussian Prime Minister Otto von Bismarck forged the unification; he was appointed the first German chancellor, while Prussian King Wilhelm I ruled as emperor. Berlin became the capital of the new German nation.

But German unity lasted little more than 70 years. Following the Second World War (1939–1945), the land was divided again, this time into two states – the Federal Republic of Germany (West Germany) and the German Democratic Republic (East Germany). It was not until 1990 that these two states were unified and Germany became a single country once more.

As a legacy of its disjointed past, modern Germany is a decentralized republic. Each of its 16 states, many recognizable as the former kingdoms, dukedoms or city-states, has its own capital. In addition, Berlin is now once again the capital of Germany as a whole.

VARIED LANGUAGES

Between Germany's different states, there is a wide variety of accents and dialects. Many of them – especially Bavarian and Swabian – are difficult to understand. The clearest and most "correct" German is supposedly spoken in and around Hanover, and on television and radio.

In the business world, however, English is more often used. This is also true in music and advertising. Music from the United Kingdom and the United States is popular in Germany, and many singers perform in English. In fact, English has become so important in Germany that children are now learning it from the first years of their education.

FIRST IMPRESSIONS

Walking through a German town, you will quickly notice a broad ethnic mix among the people. This is also reflected in the types of food available. International restaurants are abundant in city centers, along with snacks, fast food, fruit and vegetables from virtually anywhere in the world.

Typical German food can of course be found, too. German *wurst* (sausage), bread, beer and a large variety of cakes are widely available, as are locally produced fruit and vegetables. In addition, there are many regional specialities, as most areas have their own characteristic dishes.

Turkish shops and markets serve the multicultural population in Germany.

GERMANY'S IMAGE

Germany has a reputation for being very clean and orderly. Most litter bins have several compartments, each for a different type of waste, and streets are generally tidy and well kept. Even when there is a big outdoor event, such as the annual carnival, city clean-up vans move in swiftly as the last revelers leave.

Most people also think of Germany as a wealthy country with a high standard of living. Despite economic difficulties, this is still true. Many people drive expensive cars, live in modern buildings and shop for high-quality products. Cities and towns are well distributed throughout the states, and most have ample job opportunities and leisure facilities.

Many towns feature spacious squares, such as this one in Freudenstadt, Baden-Württemberg.

KEY DATA

Area:	357,021km²
Population:	82,398,326 (2003 estimate)
Capital City:	Berlin
Highest Point:	Zugspitze (2,963m)
GDP Per Capita:	US$26,600*
Currency:	euro (since Jan. 2002)

* Calculated on Purchasing Power Parity basis
Sources: World Bank; *CIA World Factbook*

A First World War cemetery, where some of the 2,530,000 German victims are buried.

Germany's status today can be traced to its actions in the twentieth century. The two world wars were fueled by German ambition, but both left the country defeated, isolated, economically ruined and politically unstable. The Cold War that followed the Second World War had Germany as its focus. It was here that the conflicting political systems of capitalism and communism clashed most directly.

THE FIRST WORLD WAR AND BEYOND

The First World War (1914–18) had terrible consequences for the defeated Germany. In the Treaty of Versailles (1919), the victorious allies imposed war reparations (compensation charges) amounting to $33 billion, which Germany could not afford. In addition, 15 percent of Germany's land and all of its overseas colonies had to be given up, depriving the nation of many wealth-producing regions.

The new constitution that Germany adopted after the First World War led to a 15-year period of political instability known as the Weimar Republic (named after the city where the constitution was established). During this time, governments were elected and then fell with great regularity. There were so many political parties that only coalition (joint) governments were possible, and these were often based on very fragile alliances. A world economic crisis during this period had severe effects. Unemployment reached record levels, the currency collapsed and ordinary German citizens endured great hardship. For this, they largely blamed the Treaty of Versailles.

THE NAZI ERA

The discontent of the German people was exploited by Adolf Hitler. He came to power by legitimate means in 1933 but soon turned Germany into a dictatorship. His demand for a strong German state, expressed through the ideology of his National Socialist (Nazi) party, had great popular appeal. Hitler believed in the superiority of a German "master race," and those who did not conform – political opponents, the handicapped, homosexuals, gypsies and, above all, Jews – were either imprisoned, deported or killed. It was, however, Hitler's desire to acquire more territory for his country (*Lebensraum*) that sparked the Second World War and, consequently, further defeat and disaster for Germany.

DIVIDED GERMANY

After losing the Second World War, Germany was occupied by the four victorious allies (the United Kingdom, France, the United States and the Soviet Union). In 1949, however, the political situation led to the founding of two distinct German states. The Federal Republic (called West Germany) adopted the capitalist systems of the Western world; the Democratic Republic (East Germany) took on the communist structure of the Soviet Union. East Germany, along with the rest of Eastern Europe, was controlled by the powers in Moscow, and the boundary that separated East from West was named the Iron Curtain. The city of Berlin was later divided physically by the building of the Berlin Wall (see page 12).

East and West Germany coexisted uneasily for more than 40 years during the Cold War period. The West, helped initially by aid from the United States, prospered (see page 34). The East remained relatively poor, with little political freedom and, for ordinary people, no chance to travel outside the communist bloc. Full employment was, however, provided by the state.

In 1948, the Soviet Union closed all land routes to West Berlin for 11 months. Allied planes, such as this Handley Page Hastings, had to be used to fly in vital supplies such as food and coal.

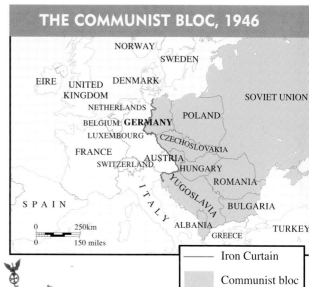

THE COMMUNIST BLOC, 1946

NORWAY
SWEDEN
EIRE   UNITED   DENMARK
KINGDOM
NETHERLANDS
BELGIUM **GERMANY**   POLAND
LUXEMBOURG   CZECHOSLOVAKIA
FRANCE
SWITZERLAND   AUSTRIA
HUNGARY
ROMANIA
YUGOSLAVIA
SPAIN   BULGARIA
ITALY   ALBANIA
GREECE   TURKEY
SOVIET UNION

0   250km
0   150 miles

——— Iron Curtain

Communist bloc

Berlin's Brandenburg Gate is a symbolic landmark. It was completed in 1791 as a monument of peace, but in the 1930s it came to symbolize Nazi power. In 1990 its meaning changed again, signifying German unity.

French sector

British sector

American sector

Soviet sector

Berlin (East)

Berlin (West)

BERLIN, 1945–49

Berlin

EAST GERMANY

G E R M A N Y

WEST GERMANY

Berlin (West)

Berlin (East)

— Berlin Wall

GERMANY, 1949–90

Berlin, today the capital of Germany as a whole, has experienced great change over the years. Having been Germany's capital from 1871 to 1945, it was divided and occupied by the four allies following the Second World War. Being under allied control should have meant:

- no German passport for Berlin's citizens
- no right to vote in parliamentary elections
- no German army in Berlin and no national service for its male population
- allied laws
- allied armed forces.

In reality, the situation was not so simple. Berlin's four-way division changed into a two-way split. West Berlin remained under allied control with the above-mentioned regulations, albeit with West German laws. East Berlin, however, became totally integrated into the communist regime of East Germany, becoming its capital in 1960. East Berliners had all the rights and duties of any other East German citizen.

THE BERLIN WALL

In 1961, life changed dramatically in the divided city when the Berlin Wall was built. In spite of separate administrations and different currencies, it was previously possible to move around freely – from East to West and vice versa. Many people, for example, lived in the East and worked in the West.

This freedom ended abruptly on 13 August 1961. Overnight, families and friends were separated and transport links were blocked. With the telephone lines already cut since 1952, communication between East and West became virtually impossible. The wall made life particularly hard for West Berliners as it turned West Berlin into an island within East Germany and its citizens into prisoners in their own city.

This separation continued for 28 years, until the wall was "opened" in November 1989. Since then, a great deal of energy, money and goodwill has gone into overcoming the division and making Berlin into one city again. Berlin became the capital of a reunified Germany in 1990.

The 154km Berlin Wall enclosed the whole of West Berlin. On the eastern side, a "death strip" was created to prevent people going near it; 160 people were killed attempting to cross to the West. On the western side, the wall became a playground for graffiti artists and, above all, a tourist attraction.

REUNIFICATION AND RECOVERY

The historic breaching of the Berlin Wall marked the collapse of the East German regime – a result of massive popular protest. But the population inevitably desired a new system of government, too. Most leaders of the reform movement wanted East Germany to remain separate and develop its own democracy. However, they were soon submerged in a popular demand for reunification. A new treaty between the victorious nations of the Second World War paved the way for this in 1990.

Reunification sparked initial euphoria, but this soon gave way to a more realistic attitude. Merging the two states has been a difficult political, social and economic exercise. Former East Germans now have to take responsibility for aspects of their lives that the state had previously managed. Consumer goods may be readily available and foreign travel accessible, but the reality of unemployment has also emerged. For the country as a whole, reunification has proved extremely expensive and there has been some resentment as the richer West has essentially borne the costs. To this day, there is a significant imbalance in the economies of the eastern and western federal states. This is reflected in unemployment levels, which remain twice as high in the East.

EASTERN GERMANY TODAY

The whole infrastructure of the former East Germany has needed to be modernized and the process is not yet complete. In the late 1980s, it was ranked the sixth-largest industrial nation of the world, but a great part of its trade was with countries whose communist economies had also collapsed, and its production methods were soon outdated. Telecommunications and transport links have now been improved and vast building projects undertaken. Equally important and equally costly, however, has been the merging of the two social systems. Working to achieve a successful joint structure for education, local government, and health, among other areas, has been problematic.

Potsdamer Platz, formerly the great crossroads of Berlin, became a desolate area during the time of the divided city. Today, its modern cafés, shops, offices and cinemas have made it once again a vibrant urban area.

The scenic landscape of Lüneburg Heath is protected as a nature reserve.

Germany's natural landscape ranges from sprawling lowland plains to rugged mountain areas, and from lush river valleys to craggy or sandy coasts. Spectacular lakes and forests punctuate the scenery. The climate is moderate to cool, with little variation across the country.

LANDSCAPE FEATURES

North Sea
North Frisian Islands
DENMARK
Baltic Sea
Rügen
Usedom
East Frisian Islands
Mecklenburg Lakeland
Elbe
NORTH GERMAN LOWLANDS
Lüneburg Heath
NETHERLANDS
Ems
Weser
Harz Mountains
Saale
Elbe
Oder
Neisse
N
POLAND
Ruhr Valley
Rhine
Eifel Mountains
Mosel
Hunsrück Mountains
Taunus Mountains
CENTRAL GERMAN UPLANDS
Main
Erz Mountains
CZECH REPUBLIC
LUXEMBOURG
FRANCE
Rhine
Neckar
Black Forest
Swabian Alb
Danube
Bavarian Forest
ALPINE FORELAND
Lake Constance
Tech
Inn
AUSTRIA
Zugspitze (2,963m)
A L P S
0 200km
0 100 miles
SWITZERLAND

THE NORTH GERMAN LOWLANDS

The North German Lowlands stretch from the Danish border south as far as Cologne, Hanover and Leipzig. The area is generally low-lying and flat, with wide plains and open valleys. In the north there are dry, sandy expanses with broad meadows, moors and heaths such as Lüneburg Heath. Northeast of Hamburg lies undulating landscape with leafy woods and numerous large, often strangely shaped lakes. The southern region, close to the Central Uplands, consists of fertile plains called Börden, where sugar beet and wheat are widely grown.

The North German Lowlands also take in the lakeland area of Mecklenburg, north of Berlin, with its low hills, forests, and more than 660 lakes. The eastern state of Brandenburg, with more than 6,000 lakes, numerous rivers and canals and prevalent woodland, falls into this region, as well.

Several large rivers, such as the Elbe, the Weser and the Ems, flow through the North German Lowlands into the North Sea. The Oder and Neisse Rivers mark the edge of the region, forming the border between Poland and Germany. Due to the extensive river network, flooding is a constant danger in this area.

GERMANY'S COASTLINE

Germany's two long coastlines also form part of the North German Lowlands. The North Sea and Baltic Sea coasts are separated only by the narrow state of Schleswig-Holstein, but despite this they are quite different.

The North Sea coastline is very flat. Gently sloping dikes (embankments) covered with meadows have been built to protect the low-lying agricultural marshland that runs along the coast. Houses here stand on small mounds – called *Wurten*, or *Warften* – that protect them against storm tides. Sandy beaches and dunes are found mainly on the numerous East and North Frisian islands scattered off the coast, all of which are popular resort areas.

Another attraction for visitors is the *Wattenmeer*, an area of sandy mudflats that surrounds the islands and stretches as far as the mainland. The *Wattenmeer* is covered by the sea during high tide, but dry with interspersed water channels during low tide.

CASE STUDY
DAS WATTENMEER

The *Wattenmeer* of the North Sea is remarkable for its immense size and beauty. It is 500km long, between 10km and 30km wide and covers an area of about 8,000km^2.

The mudflats – deposits of fine sand and clay that have settled due to the low inclination of the sea floor – stretch between land and sea. They are flooded twice a day during high tide, and they surface twice daily during low tide. At low tide, the fine surface sand is dried and blown landward by the wind, forming sand dunes and salt marshes along the coast.

Visitors love to walk across the vast, wet sands towards the open sea or from island to island. While attractive, walking here can also be hazardous due to the incoming tides.

The *Wattenmeer* is an irreplaceable habitat for many plants and animals. There are various types of cockles, mussels and worms, which are prey to a multitude of crabs, young fish and birds. The mudflats are particularly important to migrating birds as a resting place and "filling station," and they are used as a spawning ground by many kinds of fish. Other well-known animals to be found there are the common seal and the shore crab.

Walking across the *Wattenmeer* is popular with vacationers on the North Sea coast.

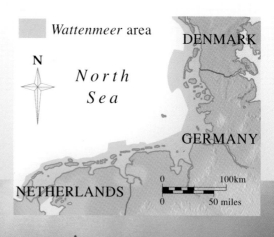

Wattenmeer area

N

North Sea

DENMARK

GERMANY

NETHERLANDS

0   100km
0   50 miles

THE BALTIC COAST

The Baltic Sea coastline is 720km long. Watery inlets called *förde*, up to 40km in length, are characteristic of the Schleswig-Holstein coast in the north. Toward the east, sandy beaches, sand bars, dunes, cliffs and lagoons dominate the scenery. This coast too is a haven for vacationers. It is ideal for water sports as well as for relaxation in peaceful surroundings. The Baltic coast is popular with families, as the shallow waters are suitable for children.

Various islands fringe the Baltic coast. The best known is Rügen, which has been a spa and holiday resort for more than a hundred years and is famous for its chalky cliffs. Today the whole island is a nature reserve. Hiddensee, a tiny island west of Rügen, remains quiet and unspoiled and boasts spectacular cliffs, sand dunes and isolated beaches. In addition, it is a bird paradise.

The third well-known island – and the most eastern part of Germany – is Usedom. This is a large island that can be reached via two bridges. It is known as the spa of Berlin because wealthy people from the capital have traditionally spent their holidays there. On the south side toward the mainland, the coast is craggy with deep bays where reeds grow on the calm shores. Less calm is the water on the

Basket chairs (*Strandkörbe*) provide protection against the wind and sun. They are a regular sight on the beaches of many German resorts.

other side of the island, which looks out onto the open sea. Inland there are large cornfields and woods, long tree-lined avenues, some very low hills (50m high), various lakes and scattered sleepy villages.

THE CENTRAL GERMAN UPLANDS

The Central German Uplands start just south of the city of Hanover. They form the core region of Germany. The rolling hills and mountains are largely covered with woods and forests and long, gently sloping valleys stretch southward towards the Danube River. The mountains here are not very high, with only a few peaks reaching 1,100m.

Other features of this area include the Harz mountains in the heart of Germany; the Hunsrück and Eifel mountains bordering the Mosel River; the Taunus west of Frankfurt; and the Bavarian Forest and the Erz mountains, both in the east. Farther south are the mountain ranges of the Black Forest stretching alongside the Rhine, and the Swabian Alb south of Stuttgart.

The Black Forest is a magnificent landscape of rolling hills and coniferous woodland.

Between the hills and mountains are long river valleys, dotted with old towns and villages. In many parts of the landscape, all of which lies at 200m or higher, a wide range of crops is grown. Dairy farming is also prominent. The climate is cooler and has more rainfall than the rest of Germany, and spring arrives late in the deep, wooded valleys. Some lower-lying areas enjoy a milder climate and are therefore ideal for agriculture.

Well-known rivers in the Central German Uplands include the Rhine, the Mosel, the Main, the Neckar and the Saale. Due to good soil and a relatively mild and dry climate, grapes (for wine) and other fruits and vegetables are grown in the valleys of all these rivers. Especially along the Rhine and the Mosel, numerous wine-producing villages have become popular tourist attractions.

Wine-producing villages are scattered along the Rhine and Mosel valleys, where climate and soil conditions are ideal for growing grapevines.

THE RHINE RIFT VALLEY

The Rhine Rift Valley carves a trough, 35km wide and 300km long, through the upland region in the west. This is Germany's warmest area, enjoying more sunshine than any other part of the country. It is an ideal climate for growing fruit, including apples, grapes, plums, cherries, peaches, almonds and walnuts.

The Rhine also forms an important water-based transport axis for north–south traffic. Anyone traveling along it will pass many large villages and towns, as well as some picturesque castles. In addition, there is a wealth of spas and health resorts running along the edge of the Black Forest, based on numerous mineral and thermal springs that rise up along the geological fault.

THE ALPINE FORELAND

The Alpine Foreland, in the south, is a long and narrow stretch of hilly land, on average about 500m high. It was formed by glaciers during the last ice age. Typical features of the area are moors and lakes set in rolling, dome-shaped hills, small villages and dairy farms.

The Alpine Foreland includes the Swabian-Bavarian highlands, dotted with large lakes such as Lake Starnberg (surface area 57km^2),

The Rhine is both picturesque and practical. A Rhine barge can transport the load of 20 trucks in a more environmentally friendly manner.

the Chiemsee (77km^2) and the Ammersee (47km^2). To the north, there are extensive flat gravel plains with pine forests, farmland and heathland. To the east, they merge into an area of gentle hills – the hop-growing region of Hallertau – and along the Danube there are fertile plains where grain crops are grown in abundance. The cultural center of this region is the city of Munich. There are also several old commercial towns that follow the course of the Danube and its tributaries.

THE ALPS

Only a small strip of Europe's Alps falls within Germany. It is about 240km long and stretches from Lake Constance (Bodensee) eastward. In this mountainous world, with its rugged peaks, steep cliffs, roaring torrents and deep glens, lie beautiful lakes and popular tourist resorts. Most of the peaks are over 2,000m high, the highest mountain in Germany being the Zugspitze at 2,963m.

The local population in the Alp valleys is heavily dependent on the tourist industry.

Thousands of vacationers arrive every year to enjoy the impressive scenery in summer and the excellent skiing in winter. Cattle and dairy farming make only a small contribution to the local economy.

THE GERMAN CLIMATE

Germany is situated in a moderately cool west wind zone, between the Atlantic Ocean and the continental climate in the east. Across the country, sharp changes in temperature are rare, and there is precipitation (rainfall) throughout the year. In summer, the temperature may vary from 18°C to 25°C, with the north being cooler than the south. Occasionally the weather may be hotter – up to around 30°C. In winter, there can be significant amounts of snow or no snow at all, and temperatures can range from –6°C up to 2–3°C, with occasional days as cold as –15°C.

The coolest areas are the mountains – especially the Harz Range – which have a particular climate with cold winds, cool summers and heavy snow in winter. The warmest areas are the Neckar, Main and Mosel valleys, with the Rhine Rift Valley having the mildest weather in Germany. A special climate also exists in Upper Bavaria with its mild Alpine wind (*Föhn*) blowing regularly from the south.

The Alps are popular with skiers in winter; tourism is a major contributor to the economy of the small alpine region of Bavaria.

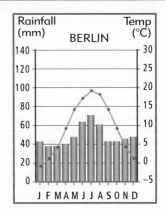

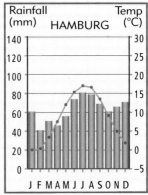

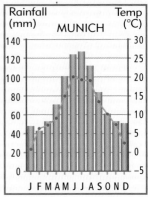

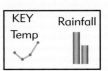

Simple roadsigns mark the national borders between Germany and its EU neighbors.

Germany is situated at the very heart of Europe. A line drawn on a map from Oslo in the north to Rome in the south will meet a line drawn from Paris in the west to Moscow in the east at a point very close to Berlin. No other European country has as many national borders as Germany, which is surrounded by nine other countries.

A TRANSPORT HUB

Germany's geographical position makes it a "transit country" – its transport systems need to cater not only to journeys that begin or end in Germany, but also to "through traffic." Trucks delivering products from Italy to the United Kingdom, for example, will have traveled along the German highways on their journey. Germany's rail and road systems are therefore vital, not just to locals but also to Europe as a whole.

The completion of the Lehrter Station in Berlin – Europe's largest transport project of the last ten years – is almost a symbol of Germany's central position. It will be the new hub of an integrated European rail network, the point at which all main routes meet.

EUROPEAN UNITY

In 1957, West Germany was one of six countries that founded the European Economic Community (EEC). This later became the 15-member European Union (EU), which expanded to 25 countries in 2004. Perhaps conscious of its unfortunate contribution to the history of the first half of the twentieth century, Germany has firmly promoted the peaceful integration of Europe. In 2002 it was one of the first countries to abolish its own currency in favor of the euro (€). The fact that the nation was prepared to give up the powerful Deutschmark was seen as a strong commitment to European unity and served as an incentive to other countries to join the common currency. Germany has also signed the Treaty of Schengen, which abolishes border controls between EU members.

This euro sign stands in the financial center of Frankfurt, home of the European Central Bank.

A FEDERAL NATION

Germany is a federal republic, just as West Germany was prior to reunification. In 1990, the former East Germany's 14 districts were replaced by five states that had existed briefly between 1949 and 1952. These are still known as the new federal states (*Neue Bundesländer)* and, together with the 11 original West German states, make up the 16-state federal structure.

THE POLITICAL SYSTEM

Each state (*Land*) has its own constitution, government and parliament and thus has responsibility for many aspects of its citizens' lives. These include, for example, transport, education, justice and cultural affairs. The states participate in national decision making through a secondary chamber of parliament known as *Bundesrat*. This body has representation from individual states in proportion to the size of their population and is able to amend, delay or even prevent laws that are passed by the main chamber of parliament, named *Bundestag*.

Representation in *Bundestag* is guaranteed to any party passing a threshold of 5 percent of the total votes, so that supporters of minor parties are more likely to feel that their votes count. Usually Germany is ruled by a coalition of a major party – the CDU (*Christliche Demokratische Union*) or SPD (*Sozialdemokratische Partei Deutschlands*) – along with one or more of the smaller parties. On occasion, there has been a "grand coalition" between the CDU and SPD. Germany's nominal Head of State is the President, whose role is largely ceremonial. The head of government, similar in position to the British Prime Minister, is the Chancellor.

Germany's parliament building is the Reichstag in Berlin. After reunification, it was renovated with the addition of a spectacular rooftop dome. A public viewing gallery inside allows people to overlook the debating chamber below.

DIFFERING STATES

Germany's states vary in size, population and wealth, with the five "new states" remaining among the poorest. The southern states of Baden-Württemberg and Bavaria combine some of the finest rural scenery in Germany with thriving industries and commercial sectors, while North Rhine Westphalia's Rhine-Ruhr conurbation, an area that includes Düsseldorf, Cologne and Essen (see map on page 46), is the traditional industrial center. Berlin, Hamburg and Bremen are known as city-states, composed of little more than these major cities and their direct surroundings.

As the German nation has existed only since 1871, it is understandable that many people think of themselves more as citizens of their state (as Saxons or Bavarians, for example) than as Germans. This manifests itself in a reluctance to move from one state to another, although there was a natural movement of labor from the poorer states of the East to the wealthier West in the years following reunification.

Each of the German states has its own flag as a symbol of its individual importance. Many public buildings fly the state flag alongside the national flag.

TRANSPORT SYSTEMS

In any modern competitive economy, efficient transport systems are essential. Germany not only has extensive road and rail networks, but is also a major hub for air travel and makes considerable use of its inland waterways as a means of transporting goods.

Only the United States' highway network is longer than Germany's 11,000km. The *Autobahn* (motorway) building program began in the 1930s as a means of moving troops and

CASE STUDY
THE A20: A CONTROVERSIAL PROJECT

One of the highways built in recent years (completion 2003) is the A20 in Mecklenburg-Vorpommern, along the Baltic Sea coast. It links the town of Lübeck with the A11 in north Brandenburg, a road that runs from Berlin to northern Poland. The new highway is 324km long and cost about €1.85 billion (about $2.33 billion) to construct.

The building of the A20 was highly controversial. On the one hand it was considered by its supporters to be an economic necessity for the underdeveloped northeast area of Germany. On the other hand, opponents of the project feared the destruction of the unspoiled environment, which is the main asset of the region.

The supporters of the road won, but many concessions to the environment were made. One example is the building of a bridge over the Uecker valley to protect its moorland. In addition, bridges for the crossing of deer, protective fences and walls for wild animals, and tunnels for amphibians were built.

military equipment quickly across the country. Although this resulted in a highly efficient road system, the German government is now actively discouraging its use by investing more money in rail and waterway transport and implementing tax measures against cars (see page 40). There are also restrictions on truck movements during the weekends as part of environmental policy. In August 2003, a traffic-reducing toll was planned, forcing goods vehicles over 12 tonnes to pay to use the roads. However, the plan was abandoned.

RAIL AND COMMUTER SERVICES

The national rail systems of the former West and East Germany were merged in 1994 under the name German Rail (*Deutsche Bahn*). The country's extensive rail network has since been upgraded. High-speed routes were introduced in 1991 with the first Inter City Express (ICE) service, and these white, high-tech trains are now a familiar sight in stations across Germany. Rail travel is further endorsed

by attractive pricing and efficient integration with other modes of transport.

In addition to inter-city rail travel, commuter services have also been updated. These are designed to ensure that people living and working in the major population areas use public transport rather than their own cars for traveling within the region. The system works well because local rail (*S-Bahn*), underground trains (*U-Bahn*), trams and buses all have coordinated timetables and switching points. Most importantly, one ticket covers all.

RIGHT: An Inter City Express (ICE) train.
BELOW: A *U-Bahn* train runs alongside Hamburg container port. Beyond the city center, *U-Bahn* trains often travel overground as well as under.

CYCLING SYSTEM

Cycling is encouraged in Germany by the provision of safe bicycle lanes in all cities. What's more, it is relatively easy to make journeys partly by bicycle and partly by rail because the trains – even the underground ones – offer easy facilities for cycle transport.

CASE STUDY
MÜNSTER – A BICYCLE-FRIENDLY CITY

For more than 50 years, the city of Münster in North Rhine Westphalia has promoted urban cycling. The policy originated after the Second World War, when Münster, like many German cities, had its center destroyed. During reconstruction it was decided that bicycles and buses should be a major part of city traffic, and routes were planned for this purpose.

Today, no other city in Germany has such a strong infrastructure for cyclists. A green, tree-lined circuit around the city center – the Promenade – is used exclusively by cyclists and pedestrians. Cyclists have their own traffic lights, parking areas and privileges on the roads, such as right of way over cars in many areas and the two-way use of one-way streets.

Children are given cycling education by the police, starting at the age of three and being tested at the age of nine. As a result of these policies and extensive advertising, Münster is now able to declare that 43 percent of journeys within the city are made by bicycle, compared to 48 percent by car. This is the highest cycle–car ratio in Germany.

People are increasingly taking to cycling as an eco-friendly alternative to car travel.

TRAVELING ON WATER

Almost uniquely in Europe, Germany has an extensive system of linked waterways. These are used for shipping loads – especially heavy goods – that are unsuitable for road transport. It is perhaps remarkable that Germany's major ports include Berlin, Cologne, Dresden and Stuttgart, all of which are a long way from the sea. This is a good indication of the extent and utilization of the inland waterway systems.

Of Germany's 7,450km of inland waterways, the most important is the Rhine River. At any point on the banks of the Rhine, barely a minute would elapse without at least one cargo of coal, stone, ore, metal waste or similar material passing by. The barges of the Rhine are vast and able to carry many times the cargo of a truck. They also provide a much more environmentally friendly means of delivery.

AIR TRANSPORT

Germany has more than 20 international airports, the chief of which is Frankfurt (am Main), one of the main airports in Europe, especially for intercontinental travel. The number continues to grow as the budget airlines now operating throughout Europe open new routes. These can give an important boost to a local economy by making use of a small or previously neglected airport. As several of the budget airlines also operate within Germany, air travel is becoming a viable alternative to railways for intercity transport.

Lufthansa is Germany's national airline.

CITIES AND TOWNS

The cities and large towns of Germany accommodate about 87 percent of the population. These major urban areas attract young people and their families because they offer the best job opportunities. Older generations, approaching or experiencing retirement, tend to remain in smaller towns and villages. In recent years, there has also been a population shift away from the former East Germany where unemployment is high. Many workers from the east commute weekly to jobs in the western cities, returning home only on weekends.

Germany's largest population center is the Rhine-Ruhr area, where 11 million people live. Other clusters appear along the Rhine, Main and Neckar valleys (see map on page 46).

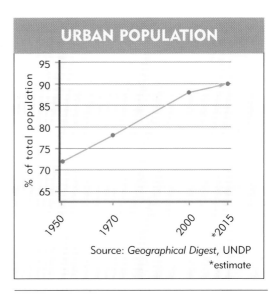

URBAN POPULATION

Source: *Geographical Digest*, UNDP
*estimate

The city of Frankfurt, beside the Main River, is a major population and business center.

Commercial crops such as barley grow in vast fields, especially in eastern Germany.

Germany is generally regarded as an industrial country. However, 30 percent of the land is covered by woods and forests, and almost 50 percent is used for agriculture. Like other sectors of the German economy, agriculture – including forestry and fishing – has undergone profound structural changes in the past 45 years.

AGRICULTURAL REGIONS

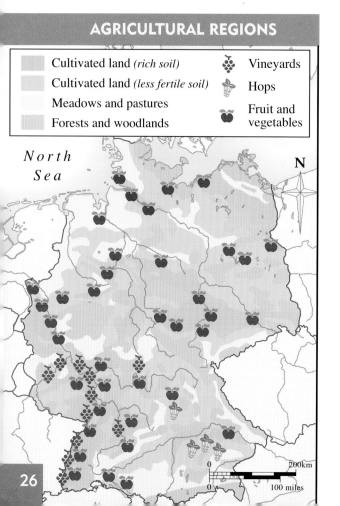

- Cultivated land *(rich soil)*
- Cultivated land *(less fertile soil)*
- Meadows and pastures
- Forests and woodlands
- Vineyards
- Hops
- Fruit and vegetables

North Sea

N

0   200km
0   100 miles

FARMING CHANGE

As in other EU countries, farming in Germany has become increasingly modernized and productive. In 1950, for example, one farm worker in the Federal Republic produced enough food for just 10 people, compared to one worker per 108 people in 1996. Today, Germany produces almost 90 percent of its own food. It ranks with France and Italy as the leading agricultural producer in the EU.

While productivity has risen, the number of farms and farm workers has dropped. In the old states, the number of agricultural employees fell by over a million between 1949 and 1997, and in Germany as a whole, there was a 30 percent decline between 1991 and 2000. By 2000, just 421,000 farms remained in Germany. Only 182,000 of these were operating full time. The others had switched to part-time farming. Many small farms have been sold or leased to those who can afford to take them on. Thus, as the number of farms has fallen, the size of those remaining has grown.

RURAL LIFE TRANSFORMED

The expanding farms in Germany generally moved out of village centers to access more space for farming equipment and storage. With the disappearance of small farms, rural villages often change their character completely. They become residential areas for people who work in nearby towns or cities but prefer to live in the countryside, which is cheaper, healthier, and provides more living space. The population structure in many of Germany's villages has changed considerably – younger people now tend to move to urban areas in search of better training and jobs; those tired of city dwelling move to rural areas to improve their quality of life.

ABOVE RIGHT: Small farms like this are becoming fewer in Germany. Many are unable to sustain themselves as profitable businesses.

BELOW RIGHT: Villages such as Oberfell in the Mosel valley thrive by selling local produce in their restaurants and shops.

CASE STUDY
THE CHANGING FACE OF FARMING IN THE SOUTHWEST

In the 1960s, farms in southwest Germany were relatively small, run by the farmer and his family, and passed down from generation to generation. Self-sufficiency was the priority, with surplus produce being sold for extra cash. Today farmers are more commercially minded; they run their farms like any other business, principally to expand and make a profit.

To succeed as businesses, farms have had to restructure. This has meant growing in size, specializing in certain products, and adopting modern technology to increase output. Farmers have had to take on hired labor in order to devote more time to managing and developing the businesses themselves.

Johannes Nägele, a third-generation farmer from Hessigheim, Baden-Württemberg, has made all these changes. Since his grandfather's time, the farm's area of arable land has grown from 18 hectares to 105 hectares, and the vineyards from 1.5 hectares to 15 hectares. He has specialized in wine and in pig farming, but where there were previously 80 pigs and 10 suckling sows there are now 1,200 pigs but no suckling sows. He buys his pigs from a specialist breeder, having stopped breeding them himself. The pigs are not fed manually, but rather by a time-saving computerized feeding system. Johannes is still a wine producer but primarily grows vines and food for his pigs. He produces pork with the help of his brother, a professional butcher, and sells it in his farm shop, together with goods that he buys from other farms.

REGIONAL DIFFERENCES

There are considerable differences in farming between Germany's old and new states. Despite changes, individual family farms still dominate in the west. These are quite small – the average farm size is 29 hectares, but many cover as little as 1 or 2 hectares.

In contrast, farms in the former East Germany were traditionally large state-owned cooperatives, run like factories by farm managers. In 1989 about 4,700 such farms existed, but after reunification they were privatized, mostly split up and reorganized. By 1998, there were about 32,000 new farms. They are all smaller than before, but still larger than farms in the west. The average size is 203 hectares, though a considerable proportion are cooperatives or limited companies with more than 1,000 hectares of land.

It is difficult to divide Germany into distinct agricultural regions, but, in general, there are more pastures in the south and west while cropland dominates in the east.

FARM PRODUCTS

As farming largely depends on soil and climate, little has changed in the proportion of Germany's arable and grassland, despite modern restructuring. The types of crops, however, have altered considerably. This is due to shifts in consumer habits and the Common Agricultural Policy (see case study). As German farmers found it ever more difficult to sell wheat and rye, they switched to fodder such as corn and broad beans, and industrial cereals such as barley and oats. They also reacted to the increased demand for meat by growing more feed plants for cattle and pigs.

LEFT: Corn is now grown extensively as animal fodder and for the production of oil.
BELOW: Vineyards dominate the slopes of the Mosel valley around the wine-making village of Pommern, Rhine Palatinate.

In many German groceries, local produce is sold alongside imported fruit and vegetables.

Increasingly, land is used for the cultivation of oil plants, particularly rape and sunflower, and dairy farming remains a thriving industry. Farmers are also encouraged to leave more farmland fallow (uncultivated), as there is an excess of food being produced in the EU.

TOP AGRICULTURAL PRODUCTS BY VALUE

PRODUCT	VALUE
Milk	€7.9 billion
Pork	€4.4 billion
Cereals	€3.5 billion
Beef/veal	€3.0 billion
Plants/flowers	€1.5 billion
Sugar beet	€1.25 billion
Wine	€1.15 billion
Vegetables	€1.1 billion

Source: Ministry for the Economy, 2000

CASE STUDY
THE COMMON AGRICULTURAL POLICY – PAST AND PRESENT

The Common Agricultural Policy (CAP) was created in the 1960s. Its objective was to increase agricultural productivity – and thus farmers' income – and to supply consumers with high-quality food at affordable prices. All this was achieved in the subsequent decades, as farmers were given government funding and encouraged to increase their output with more intensive farming. Rationalization, expansion, mechanization, specialization, pesticides, fertilizers, and new breeds of animals and crops, all became keywords.

However, the supply of important products soon exceeded demand. Quotas were introduced in 1992 to limit production of traditional crops, and milk and farm subsidies – an important part of the original policy – were cut. Other measures were introduced to promote more extensive and thus more ecological farming. Within these reforms, 8 percent of the arable land has been set aside (turned fallow).

Further changes to the CAP are under discussion. Due to the many food scandals that have shaken the farming industry in recent years – BSE (Mad Cow Disease), swine and poultry fever, antibiotics and hormone residue in meat products, for example – subsidies may only be paid in the future to farmers who deliver high-quality products and keep their animals in acceptable conditions.

The introduction of quotas hit farmers hard. Many decided to give up farming, adding to the decline in the industry. Others changed crops or switched to organic farming.

ORGANIC FARMING

Since 1988, organic farming has increased by 29 percent within the EU. There are several reasons for this development, including the granting of subsidies by the EU and national governments, a growing awareness of the environmental damage caused by pesticides and fertilizers, and many scandals surrounding farming and the overproduction of food.

In Germany, the number of organic farms has been rising steadily. Organic farming is a profitable business. While the yield is lower, the sales price is much higher. Furthermore, money is saved by doing without expensive chemicals, and the extra costs for more labor-intensive pest control (hand-checking of crops by farm workers) are compensated by government or EU subsidies.

Organic dairy farming produces less milk per hectare of pasture than conventional farming, but profits nevertheless tend to be higher.

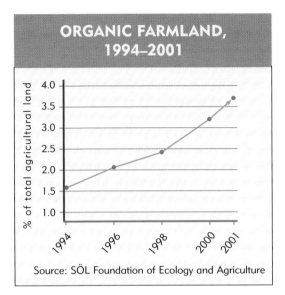

ORGANIC FARMLAND, 1994–2001

% of total agricultural land

Source: SÖL Foundation of Ecology and Agriculture

OTHER NEW TRENDS

Apart from maintaining food supplies, farming in densely populated, industrial Germany has other important functions, including:

- conserving natural ecosystems, especially the diversity of local species, the groundwater and the soil
- looking after the countryside to provide pleasant living, working and leisure areas
- ensuring a continuous supply of agricultural (renewable) raw materials – particularly rapeseed oil – for the chemical-technical and energy sector. In 1997, 4 percent of Germany's arable land was already being utilized for this purpose. Seed oils can be used in the manufacture of many non-food products, including lubricants, inks, plastics and adhesives as well as fuels such as diesel.

FORESTRY

Almost one-third of Germany's total land area is covered by forest. The two states with the most forest in proportion to their total size are Rhine Palatinate and Hesse, with about 40 percent, while the lowest proportion of forests – apart from the city-states – is found in Schleswig-Holstein, with about 9 percent.

Forestry as an industry is quite insignificant in Germany, despite the fact that home-grown timber meets two-thirds of domestic demand for wood and wood products. But forests play an important role as recreation areas for the public, especially the inhabitants of industrial conurbations. Much is done to preserve the forests and to make sure they are properly managed. The Forest Preservation Act of 1975 stipulates that forest land can only be cleared for other uses with the approval of the state authorities. In addition, it obliges woodland owners to reforest harvested areas. Deliberate measures have also been taken to increase the amount of deciduous and mixed forests, which now account for about 60 percent of the total forest area. There is, however, the additional problem of dying forests (*Waldsterben*) due to acid rain (see pages 42 and 44).

FISHING

Germany's principal fishing areas are the North Sea, the Baltic Sea, and the Atlantic Ocean west of the United Kingdom and around Greenland. Since the 1980s, the country's ocean fishing fleet has been greatly reduced due to changes in the international maritime law, which enabled coastal countries to extend their fishing zone to more than 300km offshore. This resulted in the decimation of traditional stocks due to over-fishing. Operating within the EU Common Fisheries Policy (CFP), which promotes quotas to regulate catches and safeguard species, the German fishing industry is now a fraction of its former size, and only some 20 vessels in its 2,000-strong fleet are actually oceangoing.

LEFT: Newly planted trees for reforestation.
BELOW: The Black Forest, with its quiet, tree-fringed lakes, is an attractive recreational area.

The BMW is a prominent symbol of Germany's reputation for quality products.

German is the major industrial country of the European Union and one of the leading industrial nations of the world. The country's total workforce comprises some 38 million people, representing approximately 46 percent of the population.

ECONOMIC STRUCTURE

In Germany, as in most other developed countries, jobs have been moving away from the agricultural sector for some time. Recently, they have also shifted from manufacturing to service industries, although manufacturing still provides a greater percentage of jobs than any of the various parts of the service sector.

Despite many adverse factors, the German economy remains one of the most powerful in the world. Germany is second only to the United States as an exporter of goods, and its cars and high-tech equipment are among the most desirable consumer items throughout the world. Names such as Mercedes, BMW, Volkswagen and Audi are renowned globally for their outstanding motor products, and, in technology and household goods, Bosch, Braun, BASF, Siemens and Zeiss are all at the forefront of innovation. Furthermore, the German brand Adidas is one of the best-known sports labels on the market today.

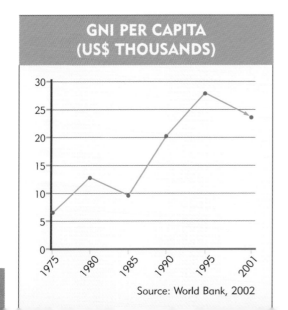

GNI PER CAPITA (US$ THOUSANDS)

Source: World Bank, 2002

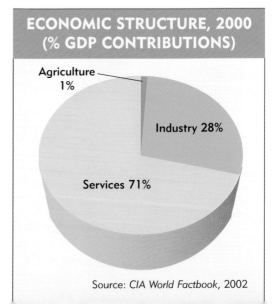

ECONOMIC STRUCTURE, 2000 (% GDP CONTRIBUTIONS)

Agriculture 1%
Industry 28%
Services 71%

Source: *CIA World Factbook*, 2002

The headquarters of the industrial company Bosch, which employs 224,000 people worldwide.

MAIN GERMAN EXPORT GOODS	
PRODUCT	VALUE
Cars	€73.5 billion
Machinery	€69.5 billion
Chemical Products	€58.5 billion
Electrotechnical Products	€42.5 billion
	Source: Globus, 1997

Germany's position as an industrial power dates from the developments in the years following the Second World War, when, from an urban landscape of almost total ruin and chaos, industries in the west of the country were rebuilt from scratch. The recovery was largely aided by money from the United States, which (under a scheme called the Marshall Plan) was distributed to help boost shattered economies throughout Western Europe.

CASE STUDY
VOLKSWAGEN AND WOLFSBURG – A DEVELOPMENT IN REVERSE

The VW factory and its theme park *Autostadt* play a pivotal role in the city of Wolfsburg.

A major industry such as motor manufacture would normally be attracted to an established center of population. In the case of Germany's Volkswagen (VW), however, it could be said that the industry attracted the town.

In 1938, Wolfsburg was little more than a village with just 1,100 inhabitants. Its central position was a critical factor in its selection as the location for the VW factory. Volkswagen means literally "people's car," and the company was to build a car that the ordinary worker could afford. The expansion of Wolfsburg since the factory was established has effectively followed production requirements. Today it is the largest car plant in the world, employing more than 48,000 workers, and the population of Wolfsburg has risen to 128,000.

The VW company, aware of its responsibility both to employees and to the environment, has always contributed to the cultural infrastructure of the town. A congress center, cultural center, theater, planetarium and museum, all designed by internationally renowned architects, are testimony to the company's importance to the city. On a more practical level, the factory's power plant supplies all of the town's heat and electricity.

In recent years, a public-private partnership – Wolfsburg AG – owned equally by city and company, has sought to reduce unemployment in the region by offering incentives to new business start-ups and by developing *Autostadt*, a theme park that showcases the company and city for an increasing number of visitors.

DEVASTATION OF WAR

In the aftermath of the Second World War, Germany was in ruins. Its great cities were destroyed and a large part of their populations displaced. Cologne, for example, had a prewar population of 750,000, but by 1946 it had fallen to 32,000. Industrial production was at a virtual standstill, and the German currency – the Reichsmark – was so worthless that American cigarettes became a more valuable means of exchange. Black markets flourished behind the scenes, and it is estimated that between one-third and one-half of all transactions at the time were by barter.

As the economy continued to stagnate, differing views regarding Germany's future were highlighted. The Soviet Union wanted to retain power over its sector, while the Western allies wished to help revive the German economy without long-term involvement. It was this conflict of ideals that led to the division of Germany into two states.

The devastation of wartime bombing is still evident in parts of the former East Germany.

ECONOMIC MIRACLE

Following the split, the economy of the West made a remarkable recovery. This was fueled initially by funding from the United States and by the willingness of Germans to work hard for low wages until productivity improved. But even more crucial were the reforms made by Finance Minister Ludwig Erhard and the launch in 1948 of a new, internationally convertible currency – the Deutschmark. This rejuvenated West Germany's economy; almost overnight the black market folded, store shelves filled and the unemployed were given the incentive to work. Although beginning from a point of near stagnation, the boom was remarkable.

Industrial production grew by 25 percent in 1950 alone and by 1960 it had more than doubled. The number of people employed rose from 13.8 million to 19.8 million, and the unemployment rate fell to near zero. Wages shot up by an incredible 80 percent between 1950 and 1955. Furthermore, social reforms such as employment rights and state health insurance were introduced, which remain the basis of Germany's welfare system today.

The Economic Miracle (*Wirtschaftswunder*) of the 1950s remains one of the greatest leaps forward made by any country, and it forged Germany's position as a leading industrial nation in the decades to come.

Economic revival meant that ordinary people could afford goods such as the mass-produced VW Beetle (seen here on display in *Autostadt*).

STEADY RECOVERY

In the 1960s, West Germany's economic growth slowed down. This was partly because the early speed was unsustainable, and partly because it demanded labor that the country itself could not supply, especially when the Berlin Wall prevented employees coming over from East Germany. The importing of foreign "guest workers" (*Gastarbeiter*) was therefore encouraged and increased substantially.

AN INDUSTRIAL BASE

The legacy of the 1950s was an economy based on heavy industry such as coal and steel production. This was the engine that drove other major industries such as the manufacture of cars and consumer goods. Although major industries were well distributed throughout the country, the main concentration of heavy industry was centered in the Ruhr region. Also significant were those industrial areas that had grown up along the Rhine, Main and Neckar valleys and in all of the larger cities.

NEW ECONOMIC POLICY

The economic slowdown in the mid-1960s led to a change of government and a different approach to economic policy. The newly elected "grand coalition" believed that, rather than allow market forces to regulate the economy, the government itself should shape economic trends. An important part of the Economic Miracle had been a social pact between employers and workers, which promoted wage restraint during the recovery period in exchange for collective bargaining rights and trade union participation. This became a key factor in ensuring that West Germany enjoyed full employment in the early 1970s.

The BASF factory on the banks of the Rhine is an example of industrial growth along the river.

The changing face of Germany's coal mining industry is documented at the German Mining Museum in Bochum, North Rhine Westphalia.

INTERNATIONAL COMPETITION

In the 1980s, West Germany's industrial output was surpassed only by that of the United States and Japan, but at the same time international competition was increasing. Major companies were merging and creating offices worldwide as the impact of globalization was first felt. The huge German car industry was challenged by the Japanese, and, as in other countries, the traditional industries of coal and steel began to reduce their labor force. In 1985, the number employed in Germany's heavy industry was barely a quarter of its 1957 peak.

EASTERN SUCCESS

Full employment was, however, always guaranteed in the state-run economy of East Germany, which also concentrated largely on industrial production. Even in the few years immediately preceding reunification, East Germany still ranked among the top ten industrial nations of the world.

A REUNIFIED ECONOMY

At the time of reunification, the economies of West and East Germany looked very similar. Both focused on industry, especially the manufacture of machine tools, chemicals, cars and precision goods. Both had a strong labor force and a high export income, although their exports went largely in opposite directions (West Germany's to the EU and the United States, and East Germany's within the communist bloc).

In July 1990, however, the economies of the two Germanys became one. It was the first time in history that a capitalist economy had merged with a communist one, although it was, in fact, more an absorption of the communist East by the capitalist West. Unforeseen problems immediately arose, of which the most severe were the comparatively poor productivity of the former East Germany and its close links with the collapsing economies of the Soviet Union and Eastern Europe.

REBUILDING THE EAST

The West German government took measures to deregulate the East German economy, and by the end of 1994 some 14,000 enterprises had been privatized. The East German mark, which was not convertible and had no international value, was exchanged for the powerful Deutschmark on a one-for-one basis; this meant, however, that wage costs in the east rose out of proportion to productivity. Businesses could not afford to keep all their workers, and unemployment was not only experienced for the first time, but also rose to very high levels.

Potential investors were often deterred by the confusion over legal ownership of land and assets, and by the country's inadequate infrastructure. Furthermore, many power stations were shut down on safety grounds, leading to energy shortages. Industrial regions were heavily polluted and needed considerable funds for cleanup. Roads and railways had been so badly maintained that they had to be virtually rebuilt, and the telecommunications networks were extremely outdated. It was no surprise, therefore, that although reunification opened up new internal markets to West German firms, most chose to expand within their existing factories in the west.

PUBLIC FUNDING

As private funds to sustain the economy in the former East Germany were not forthcoming, the government poured public money into the region to the sum of over $140 billion in the first three years after reunification and has continued to do so at a rate of $70 billion per year. This is funded in part by the "Solidarity Tax," a charge imposed on all German taxpayers to assist in the rebuilding of the east. In spite of this, the economy in the east has yet to recover completely and there has been a steady drift of the labor force to the west in search of better job opportunities.

ABOVE: Reconstruction is ongoing in parts of historic Dresden.
BELOW: Berlin's Sony Center was a costly but successful redevelopment project.

Small-scale enterprises are a feature of many industrial zones in modern Germany.

UNEMPLOYMENT, 1945–2003

Millions

5
4
3
2
1
0

1945 1950 1960 1970 1980 1990 1995 2003

Source: Globus, 1999

THE ECONOMY AND INDUSTRY TODAY

Although still one of the world's major economies, Germany has suffered both from the effects of reunification and from the changing face of world trade and industry. The government has increased taxes and sold off many of its nationalized industries (such as rail and telecommunications) to private investment. But the global economy means that production will usually flow toward countries in which labor costs are lower and there is less regulation.

The German worker has traditionally enjoyed job security, good pay and working conditions and generous state benefits, a legacy of the social pact of the 1950s (see page 35). These are now in jeopardy as new labor laws are introduced and the social security system is restructured. Germany does, however, have an outstanding record in the field of labor relations, again stemming from the social pact. The average days lost per worker through strikes is two in a five-year period, compared with 22 in the United Kingdom.

Unemployment levels in Germany remain high. In the first quarter of 2003, nearly 4 million (9.3 percent of the working population) were out of work. Paradoxically, there are serious labor shortages in some sectors, such as IT specialism and care work. This problem is being tackled by the introduction of Green Cards (work permits), which allow specialists from other countries to reside and work in Germany (see page 52).

CHANGING TRENDS

The labor market has changed its shape completely in the last ten years as the bias has moved away from heavy industry and manufacturing. Between 1990 and 2000, the number employed in coal mining more than halved, making the industry barely one-twelfth of its size in the 1950s. On the other hand, new jobs are constantly being generated. Since 1989, more than 1.5 million new jobs have been created in service areas such as information technology, consulting, marketing, customer services, leisure and tourism.

These also reflect an explosion in new business start-ups and self-employment, with more than 4 million people (almost 10 percent of Germany's labor force) now working for themselves. It is also an indication that people are becoming more mobile (moving to areas with better job opportunities), more flexible (working hours that don't constitute a "normal" working day) and even taking on two or more jobs at the same time.

Pedicabs take tourists around Berlin. These flexible, one-person businesses reflect recent changes in employment choices.

Germany's trading partners today are found mainly within the European Union and the United States. In 2002, Germany maintained a very healthy trade surplus (profit), but industrial production actually declined because it was still burdened by the massive reconstruction of the country following reunification.

With some 4 million Germans unemployed in 2003, the government launched a new program to place people back into work again. Its title is *Ich-AG,* or "Me, Inc."

One of the ideas involved is self-employment. The government offers financial incentives to people willing to start their own company. If a newly formed company has a yearly profit of less than €25,000, it receives a monthly supplement from the state. In the first year, the supplement is €600 per month, in the second year €360 per month and in the third year €240 monthly. To receive the state money, the newly self-employed worker (*Existenzgründer*) will have to pay into a pension and health plan.

Some people think this is a good strategy for lowering unemployment levels. Others say that the state help is not enough. Only when sufficient people have taken advantage of the system and demonstrated whether the subsidy makes the difference between success and failure can the scheme be fairly judged.

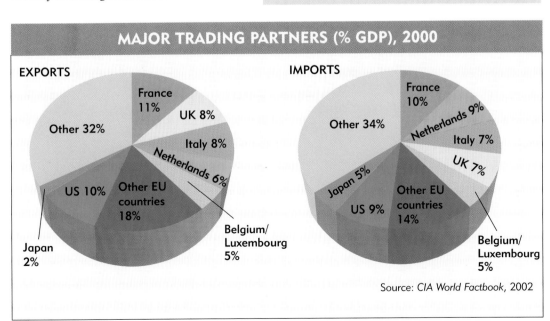

MAJOR TRADING PARTNERS (% GDP), 2000

EXPORTS

Other 32%
France 11%
UK 8%
Italy 8%
Netherlands 6%
US 10%
Other EU countries 18%
Japan 2%
Belgium/Luxembourg 5%

IMPORTS

Other 34%
France 10%
Netherlands 9%
Italy 7%
UK 7%
Japan 5%
US 9%
Other EU countries 14%
Belgium/Luxembourg 5%

Source: *CIA World Factbook*, 2002

Solar panels provide an eco-friendly means of energy consumption.

Like most industrialized countries, Germany is putting increasing pressure on its physical surroundings. Industries and households consume huge amounts of energy, draining natural resources. Urban building programs make a serious impact on the environment, as do increased travel and consumerism.

Germany has, however, taken environmental issues very seriously, especially since the 1970s when it became apparent that acid rain was killing the forests (see page 42). Awareness has also been significantly raised about cost and conservation issues regarding energy consumption; measures to reduce imports and to preserve the country's own resources have been a feature of the last decade. One example is a system of "eco-taxes," which are extra taxes on car fuel and other oils. These have been increased annually since they were installed in 1999, and the revenue raised will go toward state pension funds (see page 47).

ENERGY RESOURCES

Germany is deficient in natural energy resources and depends almost entirely on imports from abroad. Indeed, 75 percent of the nation's import expenditure is used for the supply of oil, gas and coal. In the year 2001, 97 percent of oil, 82 percent of natural gas and 54 percent of coal was imported. Although Germany still has significant deposits of coal, the hard coal of the Ruhr and Saarland

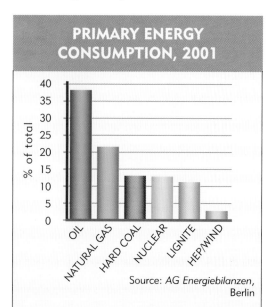

PRIMARY ENERGY CONSUMPTION, 2001

% of total

OIL — NATURAL GAS — HARD COAL — NUCLEAR — LIGNITE — HEP/WIND

Source: AG Energiebilanzen, Berlin

ABOVE: Many open-cast mines, such as this one near Cottbus, are now wholly or partly disused.
RIGHT: This old coal stripper was left as a memorial on land reclaimed from a lignite mine.

regions is expensive to mine, and the brown coal (lignite) of the east and the area west of Cologne is a serious pollutant. Lignite was the major energy source in the former East Germany. Its uncontrolled use led to severe air pollution because the power stations lacked filters; it also devastated the landscape because the mines were open-cast.

Upon reunification in 1990, the radically different systems of East and West Germany had to be merged, and the reduction of lignite mining was given priority. Production was sharply cut by the year 2000, though lignite is still an important source of electricity generation (see case study, left). Today Germany remains the world's third-largest coal-consuming country after the United States and China.

CASE STUDY
LAUBAG AND LIGNITE MINING

Before reunification, about three-quarters of East Germany's energy came from lignite. Now the industry runs at around 30 percent of its former capacity. LAUBAG, for example, a lignite-mining company based in Cottbus, Saxony, has only four out of 17 mines left.

Due to modern technology, however, productivity has improved greatly and LAUBAG now competes with the very few lignite mines in western Germany. Lignite power stations have become so advanced that they can compete with other energy suppliers, especially in electricity generation. The mines are also able to satisfy strict environmental requirements, taking advantage of government subsidies to drastically reduce pollution. LAUBAG and lignite mining will, therefore, have a future on the diversified energy market. But the new labor-saving technology means that this will never again be a high-employment industry.

NUCLEAR POWER

Germany has 19 nuclear reactors but needs to import enriched uranium to operate them. The growing awareness of environmental issues has made nuclear power a major concern, and no new reactor has entered service since 1988. The country is committed to phasing out nuclear power and increasing reliance on renewable energy.

In June 2001, the SPD/Green Party coalition government signed an agreement to shut down the country's 19 nuclear power plants. A reactor's life is now limited to 32 years and this will mean that even the newest plant currently operating will be closed by 2021. Germany is thus the first major industrial country to completely abandon nuclear energy.

FUTURE POWER

The phasing-out of nuclear power and the decreasing reliance on lignite means that greater emphasis must now be placed on alternative and renewable energy sources and also on energy-saving measures. The expectation is that up to 60 percent of the abandoned nuclear power capacity could be replaced by wind energy by the year 2030.

Wind power is Germany's main renewable resource. In August 2001, Europe's largest wind farm came into operation at Paderborn in North Rhine Westphalia. In 1999, wind power already accounted for 2.8 percent of Germany's electric power generation, and this is expected to rise to 12.5 percent by 2010.

Germany is the world's leading generator of wind power for domestic energy, producing a higher output than even that of the United States. The flat northern state of Schleswig-Holstein is already providing a glimpse of the future by producing 15 percent of its electricity requirements in this way. As suitable sites for further wind farm development are becoming scarce, the government is looking to build offshore wind parks. In 2004, a small-scale pilot project of 40 sea-based turbines was completed.

Wind turbines dominate this flat stretch of farmland near Husum, Schleswig-Holstein.

Germany is Europe's second-largest user of natural gas after the United Kingdom, but unlike the latter it has very small reserves. The only offshore field, which began production in 2000, is in the German North Sea. The country's total natural gas production has been stable for nearly 20 years, while consumption has increased by 40 percent in the same period. With natural gas accounting for 23 percent of the country's energy consumption, imports are substantial with almost all coming from Norway, Russia and the Netherlands.

POLLUTION AND CONSERVATION

In the late 1970s and early 1980s it came to everyone's notice that atmospheric pollution was killing Germany's prized Black Forest and other woodland areas. Acid rain caused by toxins in the air disrupts the chemical balance in the soil and destroys trees; visible signs include sparse crowns and yellowed leaves and needles. This realization contributed to a "green revolution" in subsequent years, as it was now clear that there was a negative side to economic success. The growth of the West German economy was bringing increasing energy demands, heavier traffic and significant urban expansion, all of which were affecting the landscape and air quality.

In addition, the former East Germany's use of lignite coal, the proximity to the heavily polluting former Soviet countries and a very large transportation sector were major causes of air pollution. In 1996, Germany's forests were damaged to the extent that only 43 percent could be considered healthy.

Air pollution was not the only problem. In the 1970s, many rivers and lakes were heavily polluted as there was little control over discharges, whether from households, industry or power stations. With Germany's major rivers all flowing northward, both the Baltic Sea and the North Sea suffered the end effect as well as absorbing direct discharges from ships and oil rigs.

EMISSION CONTROL

The German public was well informed about these problems. Consequently, the green movement grew stronger, and the government brought in a series of laws and regulations to reduce emissions from industry, power plants and motor vehicles. Many new sewage treatment facilities were constructed and

"cleaner" cars were made as the government began to base the vehicle tax on emissions produced. Reunification brought its own problems as the virtual absence of monitoring in East Germany had left some areas of heavy industry and chemical production not only polluted, but essentially poisonous.

RIGHT: Housing is threatened by pollution from a chemical plant in Duisberg, North Rhine Westphalia.
BELOW: Land reclamation work is now taking place on the sites of many old open-cast mines.

Increasing the use of public transport, including the trams that run in many German cities, is a way of reducing heavily polluting traffic.

FOREST DAMAGE

N

| 11 | Percentage of trees damaged |

SCHLESWIG-HOLSTEIN
26

MECKLENBURG-VORPOMMERN
11

LOWER SAXONY
13

BRANDENBURG
7
18
BERLIN

15

SAXONY ANHALT

NORTH RHINE WESTPHALIA
24

SAXONY
22

THURINGIA
29

HESSE
27

RHINE PALATINATE
14
25

SAARLAND

25

BAVARIA
19

BADEN-WÜRTTEMBERG

0 ___ 200km
0 ___ 100 miles

CURRENT ISSUES

By the end of the twentieth century there had been a major improvement in all polluting sectors, but traffic emissions remained a large problem. Although the introduction of unleaded gasoline, catalytic converters, cleaner fuel and better engines had produced some gains, these had been countered by the huge growth in car ownership. There are currently more than 44 million cars and 4.5 million trucks on the German roads.

Industrial water pollution has been radically reduced. Today the main damage is caused by intensive farming, whereby toxic fertilizers and pesticides drain from fields into rivers. The promotion of organic farming is now gaining ground as a way of preventing this.

The death of German forests, which is considered as a measure of air pollution, now presents an interesting picture. Although the problem has increased since the 1970s, becoming so widespread that it has afflicted almost every type of tree, there has been a steady decrease in the severity of the damage. The average proportion of unhealthy trees is still an alarming 37 percent. However, the category of "severely damaged" is greatly reducing as the health of the trees in the former East Germany steadily improves.

WASTE DISPOSAL AND RECYCLING

The emergence of the green movement in the 1970s changed the way German society perceived the age of consumerism. Previously, many goods (and their packaging) were simply thrown away after use, but people came to see this practice as destructive to the environment and wasteful of important resources.

The two chief methods of disposal were landfill and incineration. The growth of consumer spending simply created more waste, and so more and bigger landfill sites were needed, along with more incinerators to dispose of the vast "litter mountains." Dumps not only polluted water but also created a near-poisonous atmosphere in their neighborhood as their contents caused chemical reactions.

The indiscriminate burning of waste in large incinerators also led to serious air pollution.

In the early 1990s, waste management became a new and important industry, and recycling flourished. Waste is now separated at source. Public trash cans have sections for different types of garbage, and households usually have several bins so that everyone must separate waste before the regular public collections. Several times a year, each locality has a special collection of large unwanted items (*Sperrmüll*) such as furniture.

In many public places, separate bins are provided not only for different colored glass but also for cans, metal and paper waste.

Germany has found that the most effective way of controlling some types of excessive waste is financial. It is now quite normal to pay a deposit on any item purchased in a bottle, with a refund being offered upon its return. This measure has led to a substantial reduction in the volume of glass waste, and the practice has recently been extended to cans.

CASE STUDY
DOSENPFAND

Beverage bottles are stacked in crates, ready to be treated and reused.

Since 1 January 2003, German consumers have had to pay a deposit on any cans and plastic bottles that would generally be considered disposable. A law passed in 1991 stipulates that 72 percent of all drink containers should be returnable for reuse, and if the figure falls below this, action must be taken. Hence the introduction of the deposit (*Dosenpfand*).

Although three-quarters of the population agree in theory with the new charge, it is very unpopular in practice. One reason is the amount of money charged, which varies greatly from store to store. Another complication is that trade and industry have not been able to agree on a joint recycling system. As a result, the consumer must return the bottle or can to the place from which he or she bought it, which can be inconvenient. It is likely, however, that a workable solution will soon be found to the benefit of all parties.

Urban streets are frequently packed with people, both residents and tourists.

Germany is a relatively crowded country, with a total population of about 82.5 million. Nearly 9 percent of these residents are of non-German origin. The majority of people cluster in urban areas, and there are considerable differences in distribution between the states.

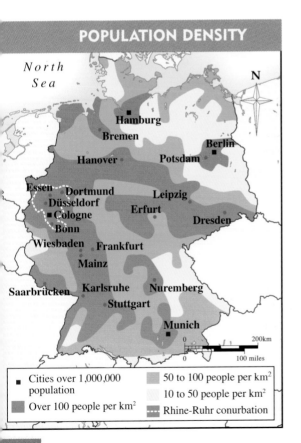

POPULATION DENSITY

North Sea

N

Hamburg
Bremen
Berlin
Hanover
Potsdam

Essen
Dortmund
Leipzig
Düsseldorf
Erfurt
Cologne
Bonn
Dresden
Wiesbaden
Frankfurt
Mainz

Saarbrücken
Karlsruhe
Nuremberg
Stuttgart

Munich

0   200km
0   100 miles

- Cities over 1,000,000 population
- ▨ Over 100 people per km²
- 50 to 100 people per km²
- 10 to 50 people per km²
- ┅ Rhine-Ruhr conurbation

POPULATION PROFILE

The German population today is characterized by its high ratio of old people to young. This imbalance has been evident for some years and is the result of a decline in birth rate and a rise in life expectancy.

As in many other developed countries, there is a tendency in Germany for couples to have fewer children than they did in the past; indeed, some choose to have none at all. Women are more likely

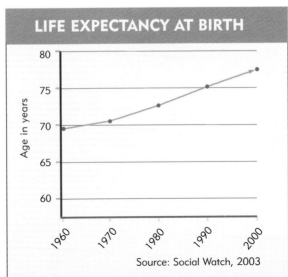

LIFE EXPECTANCY AT BIRTH

Age in years

80
75
70
65
60

1960   1970   1980   1990   2000

Source: Social Watch, 2003

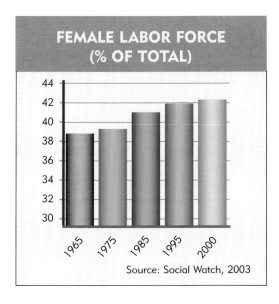

FEMALE LABOR FORCE (% OF TOTAL)

Source: Social Watch, 2003

Bad Ems is one of many spa towns whose tranquil surroundings and mineral-rich waters are ideal for rest and recuperation.

to have careers, people marry later if at all, and more couples divorce (of every 100 marriages in Germany, 46 end in divorce).

Healthier living and better medical care mean that people now enjoy longer and more active lives. As a nation, Germany is extremely health conscious. The well-being of the people is promoted by a wealth of pharmacies, health food stores, magazines, television programs, fitness centers, spas and even the concept of "wellness." This word has entered the German language as a synonym for feeling both physically and mentally healthy. An increasing number of "wellness" hotels are dedicated to health and fitness. Also significant is Germany's average of 3.5 doctors per 1,000 people. This is the fourth-highest ratio in the world and compares, for example, with 1.8 per 1,000 in the United Kingdom.

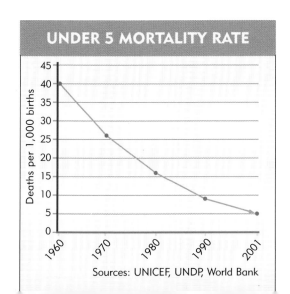

UNDER 5 MORTALITY RATE

Deaths per 1,000 births

Sources: UNICEF, UNDP, World Bank

In 2002, there were for the first time more people aged over 65 than there were aged 15 and under. A century earlier, the under-15 age group had outnumbered the over-65 age group by seven to one.

POPULATION DECLINE

Due to this swing in age profile, it is predicted that the total population will decline to about 65 million by 2050, even if an extra 5.8 million people arrive as immigrants (see page 52).

A declining population brings serious financial problems. Of particular concern is the "contract between generations," whereby the workforce of today pays the taxes, insurance and pension contributions that fund the health service and pension payments for those who have retired. In turn, this generation benefits from the next, and so on. Germany's population profile is now so biased toward its elderly members that there is a current and expected shortfall in the government revenue required for pension funds. What's more, many of today's elderly people have never contributed to the pension plan because it did not apply in the former East Germany. The eco-taxes (see page 40), although not originally meant for this purpose, are now to be used to meet the shortfall.

**CASE STUDY
POPULATION DECLINE IN STUTTGART
AND OTHER CITIES**

Retired people rely on services that are already starting to suffer due to the aging population.

In 1992, Stuttgart had 613,000 inhabitants, with the population expected to grow. In 2003, however, there were only 591,000 people living in the city. The number is likely to fall even more as the ratio of old people to young continues to rise and consequently the death rate exceeds the birth rate. In 2002, there were 110,000 people between the ages of 45 and 60, but only 15,200 between 15 and 18. An estimated 25 percent of the population will be retired by 2015.

The consequences are considerable. The city will need more facilities such as special housing, nursing homes and health care for its elderly, especially as many of them have remained childless and hence have no family to look after them. The monetary source for these projects remains unknown. The city is already losing tax income due to the general economic decline and as a result of firms closing down or reducing their operations. Schools and education facilities will close if there are no children to fill them. Change and progress cannot be brought about if there are no young people to do so.

The Stuttgart city government recognizes that the only way to reverse the trend is to improve the situation for families by offering better childcare facilities, cheaper housing and more jobs, even if they are part time. But the problem remains as to who will finance this arrangement.

IMMIGRATION

There are about 7.3 million non-German immigrants residing in Germany, making up approximately 8.5 percent of the population. This figure has remained more or less constant since 1998. Before that the number had been rising steadily.

These 7.3 million people do not have German nationality. There are immigrants who have acquired German or dual nationality since the law changed in January 2000, allowing some immigrants to be granted a German passport (see page 52). Furthermore, there are people emigrating from Eastern European countries, where their families might have lived for centuries, who are of German origin. Anyone with German blood is permitted to settle back as a German resident, and many have chosen to do so.

ORIGIN OF IMMIGRANT RESIDENTS

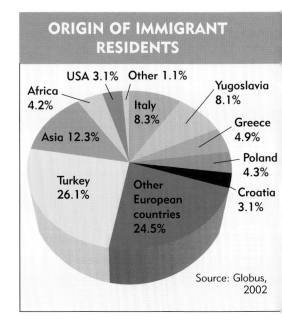

USA 3.1% Other 1.1% Yugoslavia 8.1%
Africa 4.2% Italy 8.3% Greece 4.9%
Asia 12.3% Poland 4.3%
Turkey 26.1% Other European countries 24.5% Croatia 3.1%

Source: Globus, 2002

ABOVE: Berlin's popular Turkish market is the legacy of a thriving immigrant community.

LEFT: Foreign restaurants, such as this Asian bistro in Koblenz, are a common feature of all German towns and cities.

Any person from a country belonging to the European Union can live and work in Germany. All other immigration is regulated by various laws. About 79.3 percent (5.82 million) of all the immigrants in Germany hold a European passport, including 25.4 percent who come from an EU member state. The single largest nationality group consists of the Turks, whose 1.91 million people represent 2.4 percent of the total German population. There are also significant communities of Italians, Yugoslavians, Greeks, Poles and Croatians.

Many immigrants have lived in Germany for a significant amount of time – one-third for between 8 and 20 years and one-third for more than 20 years – which permits them to apply for German citizenship. A substantial 20.9 percent (1.53 million) of people who are counted as immigrants have actually been born in Germany, albeit to immigrant parents.

THE HISTORY OF IMMIGRATION

Germany's immigration history is largely centered on the western states. After the Second World War, the Federal Republic had to import foreign workers to support its fast-developing industries (see page 35). These workers came mostly from southern European countries, such as Italy, Spain, Greece, Yugoslavia and Turkey, where there was little work and where living standards were poor. Although these so-called "guest workers" were supposed to work in Germany for only a few years and then return home, many stayed and settled permanently with their families.

ASYLUM SEEKERS

In addition, many asylum seekers come to Germany to escape persecution in their own countries. A clause in the German constitution, drawn up after the Second World War, allowed anyone suffering persecution at home to seek asylum in Germany. This created the most liberal asylum policy in Europe. The result was that most asylum seekers coming to Europe ended up in Germany; in 1990, for

example, 193,000 refugees entered Germany compared to Britain's 25,000.

The clause in the constitution was amended in July 1993 after 1.2 million refugees had entered Germany between 1990 and 1993. The changed law stipulates that only those who come directly from their home country to Germany are entitled to seek refuge. All those who travel overland must seek asylum in the first "safe" country they reach. As Germany is surrounded by such states, and most refugees must take an overland route, the number of asylum seekers in Germany has since dropped dramatically.

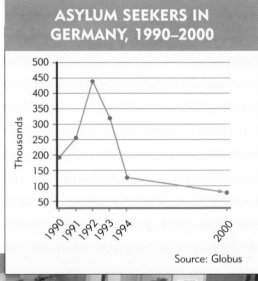

ASYLUM SEEKERS IN GERMANY, 1990–2000

Source: Globus

These Polish workers at a vegetable processing factory are not immigrants. They are allowed to go to Germany to do seasonal work.

IMMIGRANTS OF GERMAN ORIGIN

Immigration of those with German roots, whose families have lived in Eastern European countries, has been ongoing since 1950. Numbers have varied greatly from year to year; between 1960 and 1964 only 89,100 people falling into this category came to West Germany, but the 1990–1994 period saw 1,291,100 arrive. The total figure, until 1999, was 4.03 million. Since then, the yearly numbers have declined.

Although these immigrants receive a German passport upon entry into the country, they are still perceived as foreigners. They often speak little or no German and need a considerable amount of help and support. Their country of origin is generally very different, and they have problems integrating into German society. Their professional qualifications may be of little use, and many have to retrain or work as unskilled laborers.

INTEGRATION OF IMMIGRANTS

Although modern Germany is a multinational and multicultural society, the integration of immigrants has been only partly successful. In the early 1950s, Germans had very little experience living with foreign people. At first, "guest workers" had to live together in barracks, having little or no contact with German nationals. Conditions changed

Knowing the language of the host country makes life easier for immigrants. Many public and private language schools offer German classes to immigrants of all ages.

gradually, especially after 1973 when many immigrants who had decided to stay brought their families to live with them. Italian, Turkish, Spanish and Greek shops and restaurants were established. Children speaking no German had to attend German schools, and many foreign families looked for long-term places to live.

HIDDEN PROBLEMS

For years, Germans and immigrants lived side by side, not integrating but without much open antagonism. Underneath the surface, however, it was different. Immigrants often encountered discrimination when looking for jobs and accommodation. Immigrant children were seldom advised to go to grammar school to improve their prospects. It was assumed that, like their parents before them, they would only want to work in factories.

The state and the communities offered very little in terms of programs to assist the integration process. It is therefore hardly surprising that many immigrants are unwilling to give up their national customs and instead choose to live solely within their own communities.

RACIAL VIOLENCE

Due to the high number of immigrants and the many problems arising from the reunification of Germany, there was a dramatic increase in open racism and violence against immigrants in the early 1990s, resulting in many injuries and even some deaths. Although this outbreak is now long past, there is an underlying feeling among many Germans that further immigration is undesirable, and that those immigrants already in the country should integrate more.

REGULATING IMMIGRATION

Germany faces several problems if it is to oppose future immigration: It has a national shortage of IT specialists, which can only be overcome by accepting foreign workers. It also has a declining population, which could be boosted by immigrants from abroad.

An attempt to solve the first problem has been made by the Green Card regulation, which allows 20,000 people with IT skills to enter Germany for specific posts. Immigration for work purposes is, however, only allowed if no other resident in Germany can fill the vacancy, and a work permit is normally given for five years only. A new law allowing moderate immigration to compensate for the general population decline is now under consideration in parliament.

NATIONALITY LAW

German nationality is defined differently from that of many other countries. It is based on the concept of "right by bloodline" (*Blutrecht*), which means that only children of at least one German parent should have German nationality. This is why many children of immigrants remain foreigners in Germany, even if they have been born there. In other countries, nationality is granted automatically to anyone born within its boundaries.

After many debates in parliament, the German law was amended in January 2000. Today, children of immigrant parents can claim dual nationality at birth, provided that one of their parents has lived in Germany for ten years. By the age of 23 they must opt for one or other nationality.

The amendment has also made it easier for adult immigrants to adopt German nationality. If a foreigner has lived in Germany for eight years, speaks moderate German, works to support him/herself, has no criminal record and does not oppose the German constitution, he or she can become a German citizen.

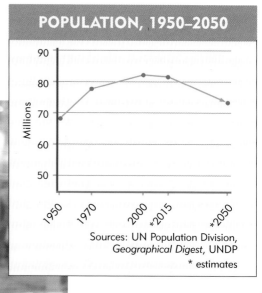

POPULATION, 1950–2050

Sources: UN Population Division, *Geographical Digest*, UNDP
* estimates

The Green Card system allows professionals from abroad to fill vacancies in Germany's short-staffed IT industry.

EDUCATIONAL SYSTEM

Germans used to be very proud of their education system until, in 2000, a comparative study among countries of the Western world revealed many deficiencies in the performance of Germany's young people. Since then the school system has been under constant review and many changes have been proposed.

Schools in Germany are controlled by the individual state authorities, so they differ slightly from state to state. It is compulsory in all states, however, to attend school full time between the ages of six and 15, and at least part time between the ages of 15 and 18.

TYPES OF SCHOOLS

Children first attend primary school for four years and then go on to one of three different types of secondary school, according to their abilities and interests. They will stay there for five to nine years depending on the type. After school, they may take either a three-year apprenticeship (vocational training with four days per week of paid work and one day's schooling) or a university degree, if the appropriate leaving certificate (*Abitur*) has been achieved. Young people today leave school later and with better qualifications than their parents and grandparents did.

SCHOOL LEAVING AGE AND CERTIFICATES		
	1980	2000
At 14/15 (without certificate)	10 %	9 %
At 14/15 (basic certificate)	37 %	25 %
At 16 (intermediate certificate)	34 %	40 %
At 18/19 (advanced certificate [*Abitur*])	19 %	24 %

Source: *Zahlenbilder*

Strolling around town and shopping are popular pastimes for young people during their six-week summer holidays.

EDUCATIONAL STRUCTURE

The average school day in Germany runs from 8am until 1pm, with homework to be done in the afternoon. However, the introduction of full-day schools is now under discussion as a means of improving student performance.

The school syllabus has seen some changes in recent years. The traditional emphasis on mathematics and German has been supplemented with subjects such as IT, science, economics and foreign languages. Teaching methods are focusing more on project work and oral expression. There have also been structural changes in some states, which vary the number of years required at each level according to the child's ability. Higher education is altering to match evolving job requirements; today training is rarely over, even if the course or apprenticeship concludes. Continuing technological advances and the growing need for specialist knowledge have made life-long learning a necessity in what is now a highly competitive world.

HOUSING IN GERMANY

The housing costs, ownership and styles of dwellings in the regions of Germany reflect the basic relationship of people to space. Major cities such as Berlin are densely populated and highly built-up, while rural areas such as Mecklenburg-Vorpommern are far more quiet and open. Housing costs are also determined by the attractions offered, such as job opportunities; infrastructure; cultural, educational and leisure facilities; geographical position and climate.

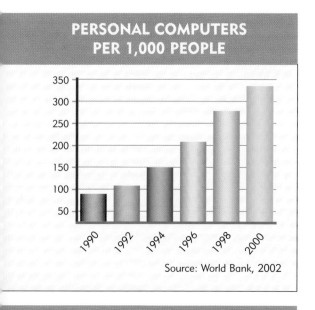

PERSONAL COMPUTERS PER 1,000 PEOPLE

Source: World Bank, 2002

TELECOMMUNICATIONS DATA

Mainline Phones	50,900,000
Mobile Phones	55,300,000
Internet Service Providers	200

(2002 Figures)
Source: *CIA World Factbook*, 2002

In Germany's large, heavily populated cities, most people live in apartment blocks or other types of old or new multistory building.

HOME OWNERSHIP

Germany's major cities are largely dominated by apartment living, typically in buildings up to six stories high, surrounding the communal space of an inner courtyard or garden. The drift of people from countryside to city for work has increased the demand for housing in urban areas, resulting in rising prices and rents. In Munich, Germany's most expensive city, a house or apartment of just $120m^2$ might cost more than $1 million to buy.

Largely because of this, most Germans rent rather than buy property. With 41 percent home ownership, Germany exceeds only Switzerland (36 percent) in Europe and compares to 68 percent in the United Kingdom. There is, however, a far higher ratio of ownership in the countryside, as a large proportion of country dwellers own the land on which they and succeeding generations build, thus reducing the cost of their homes considerably.

TRADITIONAL HOUSING STYLES

The styles of housing that most people regard as typically German tend to be found away from the major population areas. Near the northern coasts, the style is distinguished by light red brickwork and elegant, ornate gables. Farmhouses of the region are typically thatched. The distinctive black and white patterns of *Fachwerk* houses are characteristic of the central regions, while the landscapes of Bavaria and the Black Forest are distinguished by traditional farmhouses, ornately timbered and often with enormous roofs. The exterior walls frequently feature delicate paintings and the balconies and windows may be filled to bursting with geraniums.

Traditional houses with decorative woodwork still lend their charm to many town centers.

Vacationers enjoy the waterfront promenade at Warnemünde, near Rostock on the Baltic Sea coast.

LEISURE AND LIFESTYLE

In contrast to the general image of the hard-working German, the annual working hours in Germany are among the lowest in the industrial world. The average working week in Germany is 2–3 hours less than in the United Kingdom. Employees enjoy a generous average of 30 days vacation per year plus additional days for festivals, which can vary between states.

Leisure activities differ according to age group, but one of the most popular, regardless of age, is travel, whether to the beaches of the Mediterranean or to remote corners of the Earth. Germans have rightly earned a reputation for being aware of the world beyond the borders of their own country.

Sports and other community activities are also popular. A recent survey revealed that there are now almost 550,000 registered clubs and societies in the country. Together, they claim a total membership of more than 70 million people, and over 50 percent of Germans are members of at least one club. There are more than 200,000 sporting clubs, and choral societies alone have a total membership exceeding 2 million.

CASE STUDY
ACTIVITY IN VILLAGE COMMUNITIES

While German cities offer many entertainment facilities (cinema, theater, opera, clubs), it is perhaps in the smaller communities that the most individual atmosphere is found. All small towns and villages hold festivals and support a variety of organizations catering to sports and hobbies, whether it be bowling, historical societies, music or even card playing.

Rositz in Thuringia actually prides itself on being a "non-sleepy" village. Although situated more than 50km from Leipzig, the nearest city, its 3,000 inhabitants have many possibilities to enjoy an active social life. There is, for example, a sports club, a choral society, a fishing club, a military veterans association, a CB radio group, allotment societies, poultry- and rabbit-breeding clubs, a stamp-collecting club and an association of exiles from other countries. In keeping with small community tradition, Rositz also has a voluntary fire brigade whose members provide the local brass band, an important feature of the regular carnivals and festivals that the village holds.

ABOVE: Sailing clubs, such as this one on the Mosel, encourage active leisure pursuits.
LEFT: Landscaped, traffic-free zones provide relaxing surroundings within many city centers.

INTEREST IN THE MEDIA

Watching television is a highly popular leisure activity in Germany. Since 1985, both private and public broadcasting have been available. Public television and radio organizations receive their income from a user fee and limited advertising, and each channel is obliged to offer an equal share of educational, cultural and entertainment programs.

Newspapers are also widely read; most of them are regional, with a section dedicated to local news in addition to national and international reports. Many households subscribe annually to their favorite newspaper. Only a few German papers have a truly national circulation, the most popular being *Bild*, a tabloid that concentrates largely on sensational stories and has an unusually high ratio of pictures to text.

GERMANY'S FUTURE

Germany today is still in the process of harmonizing the remaining differences between the former East and West. In 1990, experts predicted that the total merging of the two previously opposed states would require a generation to complete, and Germany is barely halfway along that road.

While continuing to be one of the strongest economies of modern times, Germany is also experiencing many of the problems apparent throughout the industrial world. Globalization has contributed to increasing unemployment, and the aging population continues to feed a crisis in social welfare costs.

But above all, Germany remains committed to Europe. More than any other country, it has regarded its own interests as secondary to the principle of European unity. Germany continues in its efforts to make both national reunification and the integration and expansion of the European Union a success.

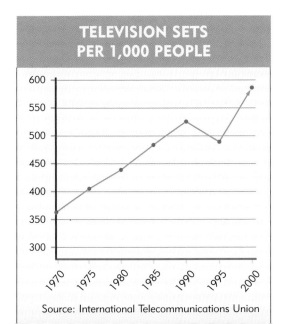

TELEVISION SETS PER 1,000 PEOPLE

Source: International Telecommunications Union

Asylum seekers People who seek refuge in a foreign country because they have suffered persecution in their native land.

Autobahn A highway.

Birth rate The number of children born in a year per 1,000 population.

Black market Illegal trading in goods, services or currency, usually during a time of shortages.

Bundesrat The second chamber of parliament, with representation from every state according to its population. It must approve laws that affect the whole of the republic.

Bundestag The law-making chamber of parliament.

Capitalism A political and economic system in which private capital or wealth is used for production and distribution.

Coalition A government that is formed by an alliance between two or more political parties.

Cold War The period of conflict between the Western powers and the Soviet Union and its allies in the decades following the Second World War. It concluded with the fall of the Berlin Wall in 1989, although various treaties had improved international relations since the 1970s. The divided Germany was often the focal point of the tension.

Communism A political and economic system based on state control and common ownership of land and production facilities and resources.

Communist bloc The countries of Eastern Europe (behind the Iron Curtain) that were controlled by the Soviet Union in the period from the end of the Second World War to 1990.

Constitution The agreed-upon basic principles of a national government.

Conurbation A large urban area created when several towns grow together.

Death rate (also called mortality rate) The number of people who die in a year per 1,000 population.

Deutschmark The currency of West Germany from 1949, and of Germany as a whole from 1990, until the introduction of the euro in 2002.

Economic Miracle (*Wirtschaftswunder*) The dramatic recovery and success of the West German economy that occurred in the 1950s.

European Union (EU) The countries that have joined together to achieve closer political, economic and social cooperation within Europe.

Federal Republic of Germany (FRG, or *Bundesrepublik Deutschland, BRD*) The area commonly known, until 1990, as West Germany. Now the correct name for Germany as a whole.

Föhn A warm wind prevalent in the south of Germany.

Förde Drowned valleys created when water flowed under the former ice margins of north Germany.

GDP (Gross Domestic Product) The total monetary value of goods and services produced by a country in a single year.

German Democratic Republic (GDR) Commonly referred to as East Germany. It was replaced in 1990 by the five new federal states of the current, reunified, Federal Republic of Germany.

Globalization The process of large corporations establishing themselves in a number of different countries.

GNI (Gross National Income) Sometimes called the Gross National Product, or GNP, this is the total value of goods and services produced by a country, plus any earnings from overseas, in a single year.

Guest workers (*Gastarbeiter*) Foreign workers who were invited to come to West Germany in the period between 1955 and 1973 to make up for labor shortages.

Infrastructure The political, communications and service systems supporting an economy and society.

Lebensraum Literally, "space to live." The expression was used in the Nazi era to explain Hitler's desire to gain more territory for the German people.

Marshall Plan Financial assistance given by the United States to countries of Western Europe to assist in reconstruction after the Second World War.

Nazi The name of the socialist party led by Adolf Hitler. The word is also used to describe the era of Hitler's power (1933–1945) and the ideology behind his rule.

Prussia The largest and most dominant of the kingdoms, dukedoms and city-states that unified to form Germany in 1871. Prussia covered a large area in the north of the land we now call Germany.

Quota A form of control or rationing that establishes a limit, such as the amount of grain or milk that a farm may produce in a year.

Republic A country or state that does not have a monarch or reigning family.

Rift valley A valley with steep, roughly parallel sides, formed by a rift in the Earth's crust.

S-Bahn Commuter trains linking city centers with the suburbs.

Spa A town that offers health-improving qualities, such as mineral-rich waters or unpolluted air.

U-Bahn (*Untergrundbahn*) The train system that runs within major cities, usually underground.

War reparations Compensation paid by one country to another for losses sustained during a war.

Wattenmeer The North Sea coastal area that is a stretch of land during low tide and a stretch of sea during high tide. Today it is a nature reserve.

Weimar Republic The period (1918–1933) between the end of the First World War and the Nazi era. It was so called because the new constitution was drawn up in the city of Weimar.

FURTHER INFORMATION

BOOKS TO READ:

Cooke, Tim. *Germany (Fiesta!)*. London: Watts Publishing Group, 1997.

Facts About Germany. Frankfurt am Main, Germany: Societats-Verlag, 1996.

Ganeri, Anita. *Germany and the Germans* (Focus on Europe). London: Watts Publishing Group, 2001.

Heneghan, Tom. *Unchained Eagle: Germany after the Wall*. Upper Saddle River, NJ: Pearson Education, 2000.

Levy, Patricia. *The Fall of the Berlin Wall*. Oxford, England: Raintree Publishers, 2002.

Lord, Richard. *Culture Shock! Germany: A Guide to Customs and Etiquette*. Portland, OR: Graphic Arts Center Publishing Company, 2003.

Pollard, Michael. *Great Rivers: Rhine*. London: Evans Brothers, Ltd., 2002.

WEBSITES:

www.destatis.de
The statistical records of the German government.

http://lcweb2.loc.gov
The Library of Congress, with comprehensive facts on all countries of the world.

www.cia.gov/cia/publications/factbook
The Central Intelligence Agency's online factbook, with statistics and assessments of all countries of the world.

www.germanculture.com.ua
An informative source of articles on all aspects of life in Germany.

www.german-embassy.org.uk
Information on German politics and current affairs.

www.germany-tourism.de/
Information on German history and the federal states as well as facts on tourism.

www.goethe.de
Website of the official organization for the promotion of German language and culture. Includes many useful links to other sites.

METRIC CONVERSION TABLE

To convert	to	do this
mm (millimeters)	inches	divide by 25.4
cm (centimeters)	inches	divide by 2.54
m (meters)	feet	multiply by 3.281
m (meters)	yards	multiply by 1.094
km (kilometers)	yards	multiply by 1094
km (kilometers)	miles	divide by 1.6093
kilometers per hour	miles per hour	divide by 1.6093
cm^2 (square centimeters)	square inches	divide by 6.452
m^2 (square meters)	square feet	multiply by 10.76
m^2 (square meters)	square yards	multiply by 1.196
km^2 (square kilometers)	square miles	divide by 2.59
km^2 (square kilometers)	acres	multiply by 247.1
hectares	acres	multiply by 2.471
cm^3 (cubic centimeters)	cubic inches	multiply by 16.387
m^3 (cubic meters)	cubic yards	multiply by 1.308
l (liters)	pints	multiply by 2.113
l (liters)	gallons	divide by 3.785
g (grams)	ounces	divide by 28.329
kg (kilograms)	pounds	multiply by 2.205
metric tonnes	short tons	multiply by 1.1023
metric tonnes	long tons	multiply by 0.9842
BTUs (British thermal units)	kWh (kilowatt-hours)	divide by 3,415.3
watts	horsepower	multiply by 0.001341
kWh (kilowatt-hours)	horsepower-hours	multiply by 1.341
MW (megawatts)	horsepower	multiply by 1,341
gigawatts per hour	horsepower per hour	multiply by 1,341,000
°C (degrees Celsius)	°F (degrees Fahrenheit)	multiply by 1.8 then add 32

Silhouetted trees in the Black Forest.